# I'M GOOD AT
# DESIGN &
# TECHNOLOGY
## WHAT JOB CAN I GET?

Richard Spilsbury

WAYLAND

First published in 2013 by Wayland
Copyright © Wayland 2013

Wayland
338 Euston Road
London NW1 3BH

Wayland Australia
Level 17/207
Kent Street
Sydney, NSW 2000

Produced for Wayland by
White-Thomson Publishing Ltd
www.wtpub.co.uk
+44 (0)843 2087 460

Commissioning editor: Victoria Brooker
Project editor: Kelly Davis
Designer: Tim Mayer
Picture research: Richard Spilsbury
Proofreader and indexer: Lucy Ross

Dewey categorisation: 745.2'023-dc23

ISBN-13: 9780750280099

Printed in China

10 9 8 7 6 5 4 3 2 1

Wayland is a division of Hachette
Children's Books, an Hachette UK company.
www.hachette.co.uk

## Picture credits

1, Shutterstock/pryzmat; 3, Dreamstime/
Garcea; 4, Dreamstime/Rkaphotography; 5,
Dreamstime/Hongtao926; 6, Dreamstime/
Daikunhong; 7, Dreamstime/Ragsac19; 8,
Dreamstime/Kelvintt; 9, Shutterstock/Viktoriya;
10, Shutterstock/auremar; 11, Dreamstime/
Abc4foto; 12, Dreamstime/jkirsh; 13,
Dreamstime/Simonovics; 14, Dreamstime/
Garcea; 15, Dreamstime/Dalesemt; 16,
Dreamstime/Supertramp; 17, Shutterstock/
jamiehooper; 18, Dreamstime/Ptimages2;
19, Dreamstime/Dimjul; 20, Shutterstock/
Leah-Anne Thompson; 21, Shutterstock/
amenic181; 22 Dreamstime/Luoxubin; 23,
Shutterstock/pryzmat; 24, Shutterstock/
Monkey Business Images; 25, Shutterstock/
Belushi; 26, Shutterstock/Diego Cervo; 27,
Shutterstock/catwalker; 28, Dreamstime/
Punkle; 29, Shutterstock/Pixel 4; cover
(top left), Shutterstock/Goodluz; cover (top
right), Shutterstock/thieury; cover (bottom),
Shutterstock/Viktoriya.

## Disclaimer

# CONTENTS

# The world of design and technology

Imagine having the idea for the iPad, the look of a new restaurant chain, or a piece of clothing worn by thousands of people. These are just some of the concepts thought up by people who work in design and technology (D&T).

## The importance of design and technology

Design affects everything in our lives, from bin bags and sports shoes to chairs and houses. Without designers, objects might look unappealing, fail to work, or be made of unsuitable materials. But design is nothing without technology. The application of technology (ranging from properties of materials to recyclability) enables designers to create useful and life-enhancing products.

↓  An elite cyclist owes part of their success to high-tech bikes developed by people with D&T skills.

← The iPad is a blend of cool design and easy-to-use technology that has captivated shoppers worldwide.

## D&T in the workplace

There are many D&T-related careers across a wide range of industries, including, for example, agriculture, construction, architecture, engineering, healthcare, fashion and food. Skills, such as understanding the limitations and properties of materials, and training in computer-aided design (CAD) and computer-aided manufacturing (CAM) software, are in great demand. They enable people to design and manufacture anything – whether it's a tasty ready-cooked meal or a new generation of spacecraft.

## Special skills

People who are good at D&T are usually very creative and inventive. They are capable of following an idea through from design to actual use by asking and answering questions such as: 'Who will use the product?', 'What materials should I use?' and 'How will the product affect the environment (its sustainability)?' Studying D&T requires logical thinking, problem-solving, team work, research, IT knowledge and planning. Read on to find about some of the jobs for people with D&T skills.

**PROFESSIONAL VIEWPOINT**
'The world faces a huge shortage of engineers with hands-on experience designing, making and using modern tools such as CAD/CAM, electronics and control systems. Exciting and imaginative D&T teaching in school will be crucial for our future success.'
Andrew Renouf, personnel manager

# Model maker

Have you always liked making models – from building bricks to college design projects? Then you might enjoy doing it professionally! Model makers design and make models to show how buildings or products will look, or to test what it is like to use them in reality.

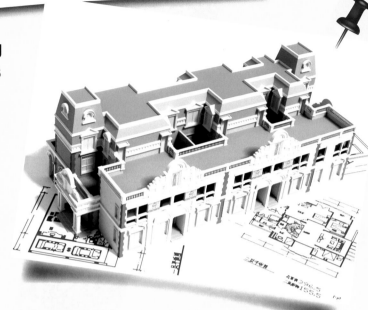

Model makers need patience and technical skills to create accurate scale models.

## Different types of model maker

Model makers create three-dimensional (3D) scale models, using a variety of media such as wood or clay. They may make models to show the general shape or concept for a new product, or they may provide a detailed, functioning prototype. Some model makers specialise in particular industries. For instance, they could make models for architects or models for use in special effects for TV and film productions.

### Job description

## Model makers:
• plan models to a brief, which sets out the criteria for design, based on client requirements and constraints including price and timescale
• use freehand drawing skills or CAD to illustrate initial ideas
• produce detailed final models, following consultation on any necessary changes
• use a range of materials and appropriate tools and machines
• incorporate electronics and mechanics to make working models
• add finishing touches such as spray painting.

# What skills do I need?

Model makers need good drawing and IT skills, and the ability to convert flat plans and technical drawings into objects. Most of them have qualifications from a college or university course like model making and design modelling, design crafts, or integrated 3D design. It should help you get onto a course if you put together a portfolio of any models you make at school, college or for your own interest, and the design briefs you followed.

## PROFESSIONAL VIEWPOINT

'You need to be able to think spatially to look at a two-dimensional drawing and add in the third dimension. Most model makers can see something on paper and know what it will look like if it is flipped over or turned in space.'

**Duane Martinez, model maker**

↑ Model makers may use computer-aided manufacturing software to make simple models.

# Interior designer

Do you like being in your bedroom at home? The appearance and layout of a room can make a big difference to whether we feel comfortable in it. Interior designers plan and supervise the design and decoration inside buildings.

The choice of fittings, colours and decorations in a restaurant can affect whether or not customers choose to eat there.

## Job description

### Interior designers:
- discuss a client's ideas, requirements and budget to create a brief
- make sketches of initial ideas to meet the brief and submit them to the client for approval
- advise and present samples of colour schemes, fabrics, fittings and furniture
- create detailed drawings from the sketches and prepare accurate costings
- carry out the design, liaising with tradespeople (such as painters, decorators, upholsterers and carpet layers) where necessary.

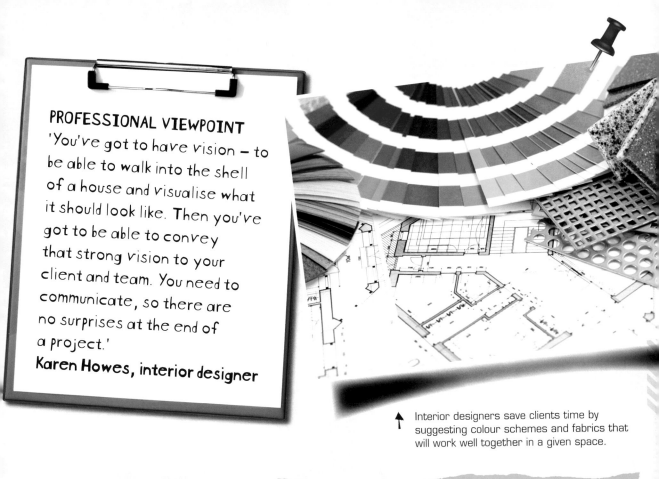

Interior designers save clients time by suggesting colour schemes and fabrics that will work well together in a given space.

## Different types of interior designer

Some interior designers are hired to design a single room or floor of a private home or office space. Others plan the whole interior of new buildings such as apartment blocks, from the shape and layout of rooms, to choosing paint colours and light fittings. Some interior designers specialise in domestic or private projects and others in commercial or public buildings, from restaurants and museums to offices and banks.

## What skills do I need?

An interior designer needs to be creative and practical, and an excellent communicator and organiser to ensure that clients get the designs they want, within the agreed budget and timescale. Interior designers usually have an art or design-based BTEC HND or degree to gain skills in drawing, CAD and model making. They need to keep up with changing trends in the colours and materials used in interiors, and have an understanding of design constraints such as building and safety regulations.

# Electrician

We all take electricity for granted, but imagine any home, school or community without it – powering everything from lights and computers to heating and air conditioning systems. Electricians plan and install electrical systems, usually in buildings.

↑ Electricians need training so that the wiring and electrical components they put in are safe to use.

## Job description

### Electricians:
• plan the layout and installation of wiring, equipment and fixtures to meet clients' wishes and safety regulations
• connect wires to a variety of electrical components, from power sockets to computer systems
• inspect, test and fix faults or hazards in existing electrical systems
• keep up to date with changing electrical regulations and qualifications
• find clients and discuss electrical solutions that will meet their needs.

## Different types of electrician

Some electricians mainly work in people's homes – for example, putting in power sockets and wiring. Others specialise in installing and maintaining power, lighting or data networks in offices, or street lights and information signs on roads, or high-voltage electrical equipment in power stations. Some electricians are electrical engineering technicians. They implement designs for whole electrical systems made by electrical engineers, such as cables from a new wind farm or lighting for a new sports stadium.

## What skills do I need?

Electric shocks are potentially deadly, so electricians must pay close attention to detail to maintain safety. Many start by studying BTECs at college or becoming apprentices after school, working towards an NVQ. They may later take HNDs or HNCs, which can lead to well-paid electrical engineering technician jobs. Good ICT, physics and maths skills are very useful to complete all the qualifications. Electrical engineers usually take a degree in electrical engineering.

↑ Electrical engineers design systems for large, often complicated projects.

# Product designer

Sandwich toasters, wind-up radios and mobiles look and work as they do because of product designers. These designers develop, make and test a wide range of products that are in use every day.

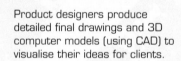

← Product designers produce detailed final drawings and 3D computer models (using CAD) to visualise their ideas for clients.

## Different types of product designer

Some product designers work for companies that design a wide range of products. Others work on a narrower range. For instance, they may design specialised products to make life easier and safer for people with mental difficulties (such as those caused by dementia). Some designers develop and test new materials to make products more resilient, cheaper or easier to recycle. They are sometimes called product engineers and they may work closely with engineering companies and factories to adapt their designs, making them easier to manufacture.

## Product designers:

- create and work to briefs for new products in consultation with clients
- plan projects through several stages, working out prices and budgets
- do initial sketches and decide on suitable materials for designs
- make prototypes, sometimes working with model makers or specialist engineers
- test designs and find solutions to problems, often in teams.

↓ Whether it is a laptop or a screwdriver, people rely on product designers to create objects that are both functional and visually appealing.

## What skills do I need?

Product designers aim to produce things that are attractive, reliable, and easy to maintain and use, while taking into account constraints such as costs, safety and sustainability. Key to this is an understanding of material properties, and how products are manufactured.

Many product designers take degrees or HNDs in product, industrial or 3D design. A wide-ranging portfolio, demonstrating ideas that solve problems and meet design briefs, could help you get onto this type of course.

# Technical textiles designer

Think about the waterproof and breathable jackets worn by mountaineers, the compression vests worn by sportspeople, and clothes that can change colour in sunlight. The special functional properties of the fibres and fabrics in these and many other products were all designed and developed by technical textiles designers.

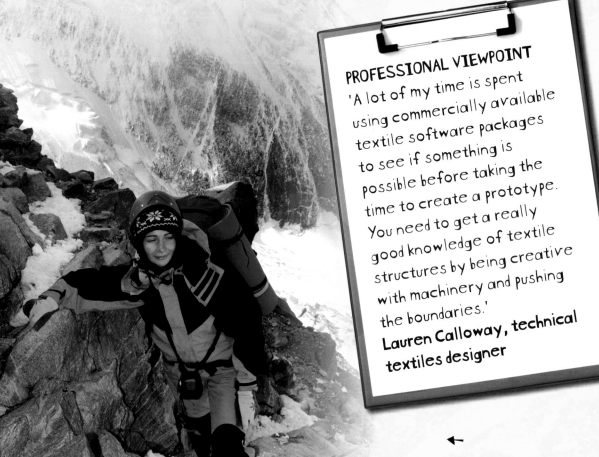

**PROFESSIONAL VIEWPOINT**
'A lot of my time is spent using commercially available textile software packages to see if something is possible before taking the time to create a prototype. You need to get a really good knowledge of textile structures by being creative with machinery and pushing the boundaries.'
**Lauren Calloway, technical textiles designer**

←

Technical fabrics in mountaineers' clothes protect them from their harsh surroundings, and even help them survive if weather conditions get bad.

# What skills do I need?

It really helps to understand how and why people have improved the functions and properties of textiles in the past in order to think of further improvements. Technical textile designers often study chemistry and physics at school or college and take a degree in textiles or textile technology to learn about the science, manufacturing processes, and textile industry. They may then gain experience working for a company and complete qualifications offered by the Textile Institute.

↓
Firefighters' clothing is made from fire-resistant fabric, which protects them from very high temperatures.

## Different types of technical textile designer

Some designers develop technical textiles for high-performance clothing. For example, the fabric of a bulletproof vest worn by soldiers needs to be light and flexible but also able to stop bullets. Some design textiles for the health or medical industries, such as artificial parts used by surgeons to mend joints. Others may create textiles that cover light aircraft wings or protect buildings from earthquake damage.

### Job description

## Technical textile designers:
- design innovative textiles, sometimes to a client's brief
- produce a range of designs and help develop product prototypes
- test the prototypes in the laboratory and in real-life situations to assess their performance
- record and analyse test results, and write technical reports on products
- keep up to date with new materials, research techniques and technologies.

# Carpenter

Wood is one of the oldest raw materials known to man. It has been used for centuries to create objects, from functional shelters to works of art. If you like making things using wood, becoming a carpenter could be an ideal career for you.

## — Job description

### Carpenters:

- design wooden objects and structures to a client's brief, advising on appropriate woods for particular purposes
- use a wide range of hand tools, such as saws and power tools (including sanders), to cut and shape wood
- use a variety of fixing and jointing techniques to assemble structures
- choose and apply materials (like varnishes) to protect wood
- restore damaged parts of wooden structures
- use safety techniques to reduce hazards such as breathing in sawdust and injury from sharp tools.

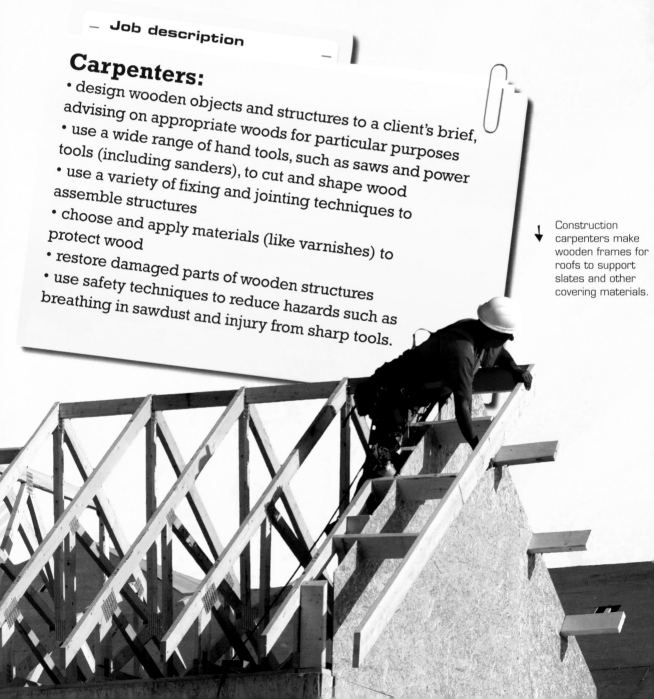

Construction carpenters make wooden frames for roofs to support slates and other covering materials.

Carpenters and joiners work widely in the construction industry. For example, they make and install windows and doors, and create wooden formwork to support concrete that is setting. Some carpenters specialise in making wooden interiors for shops, banks and other public buildings. Others become boat builders or cabinet makers, producing fine wooden furniture including sideboards and chairs. Carpenters work in a variety of settings, in factories, workshops or outdoors.

Luthiers are specialist carpenters who create and mend double basses, wooden guitars and other stringed instruments.

### PROFESSIONAL VIEWPOINT

'Being a carpenter is not only about pounding nails; it also involves good communication skills, an appreciative eye, a thorough knowledge of materials and best practices and the ability to complete a job. Perhaps the most important element is to be able to communicate well.'

**Omar, independent carpenter**

## What skills do I need?

A carpenter needs to be practical and artistic, but also mathematical and scientific – for instance, to work out angles, measure lengths and calculate the ability of wooden beams to support a certain weight. Carpenters should be able to work alone and as part of a team, especially on a construction site. Many carpenters become apprentices to gain experience, and gain BTEC qualifications to develop their skills.

# Jewellery designer

Jewellery can be incredibly beautiful and is produced by skilled individuals. If you are creative, have an interest in styles and designs of jewellery, and are good at making accurate, detailed objects, then this job might suit you.

## Job description

### Jewellery designers:

- create jewellery designs as drawings or computer simulations
- consult clients on the style and materials to be used in commissions
- choose and source metals, gemstones and other materials, based on their quality, properties and cost
- use a variety of techniques (like cutting, hammering, soldering and polishing) to produce finished pieces
- mend or adapt existing jewellery, such as resizing rings
- market and sell their jewellery in shops, fairs and online.

← A jewellery designer often creates and sells designs from their workshop.

## Different types of jewellery designer

Some jewellery designers work for large companies, designing jewellery that is then made by other people. But most jewellery designers are self-employed, making individual pieces to their own designs and also to those requested by clients. Some jewellery designers also run courses to teach others how to make jewellery.

It requires patience and skill to create unusual, attractive pieces of jewellery.

## What skills do I need?

You will need artistic ability and great attention to detail – the work is often fiddly and materials for jewellery are usually expensive, so losing or damaging them while working can be very costly. Many jewellers have a foundation degree, BTEC HND or degree in a subject such as jewellery design or designed metalwork. It is really useful to take a short course at a jewellery studio or workshop to see if it is the job for you, and to start to learn some techniques.

PROFESSIONAL VIEWPOINT

'Craft skills don't arrive overnight. Techniques can be learnt in a couple of days but to become really proficient at a craft you have to put the time in. I try to encourage my students not to rush, but enjoy the learning process, as this tends to carry on throughout life anyway.'

Jesa, jewellery designer and maker

# Food technologist

Have you ever wondered who comes up with new types of chocolate bars and who designs the airtight packaging for soup or fruit juice? Food technologists develop and present a wide range of food and drink in ways that tempt people to buy them, while making sure that the products stay safe and fresh.

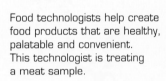

Food technologists help create food products that are healthy, palatable and convenient. This technologist is treating a meat sample.

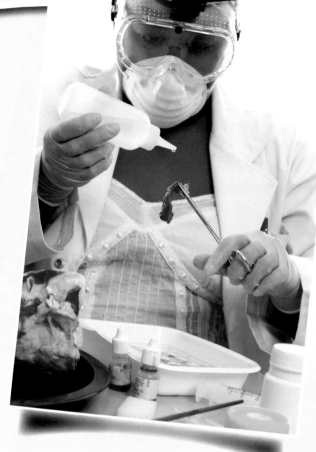

## Job description

### Food technologists:
- design packaging for specific foods
- research consumer markets to develop products
- make and test samples
- ensure that food safety standards are followed
- identify, choose and price products from suppliers
- liaise with factories that manufacture products
- check and improve quality control and hygiene procedures in factories.

## Different types of food technologist

Food technologists work in kitchens, factories, laboratories and offices. Some work with manufacturers, designing and developing packaging to protect and preserve foods and drinks. Others create new recipes or use ingredients to develop improved types of food, such as fat-free products or ready meals. They may also design machinery and processes for making the products in large quantities in factories. Some food technologists are quality controllers who check that factories prepare food products safely and to the required standard.

# What skills do I need?

Most food technologists have a BTEC HNC or HND or a degree in a subject like food technology, in which they learn about topics such as chemical engineering, production planning, and market and consumer research. The job is very 'hands on' so you need to enjoy cooking and making objects, but also getting involved in solving production problems and motivating other team members who may be working on new products.

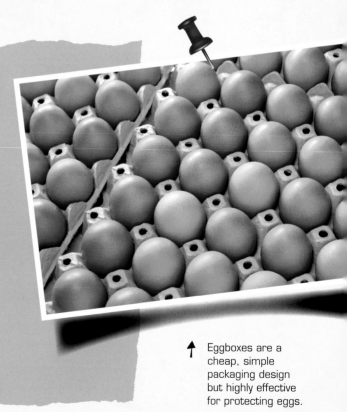

↑ Eggboxes are a cheap, simple packaging design but highly effective for protecting eggs.

# Structural engineer

Most of the big structures you see around you, including houses, theatres, sports venues and hospitals, and even those you cannot usually see – like space satellites – were designed by structural engineers.

## Job description

### Structural engineers:

- discuss projects with clients and architects
- develop design ideas, using CAD, and advise on suitable materials
- work out loads and stresses on parts of a structure such as foundations and walls
- use computer modelling to test how buildings will react, for example in high winds or earthquakes
- make drawings, specifications and computer models of structures for builders
- inspect unsafe buildings and suggest ways of repairing them
- make sure projects are safe and meet legal and environmental guidelines
- supervise project teams and report to clients and managers.

→ The challenge for structural engineers is to create buildings that are strong, durable and safe but also have eye-catching, striking designs.

Structural engineers design structures to withstand stresses and pressures, such as severe weather conditions. They make sure buildings and other structures are constructed using materials that remain strong and secure. They also inspect existing buildings to test whether they are structurally sound and safe. Structural engineers liaise with architects, builders and many other construction professionals.

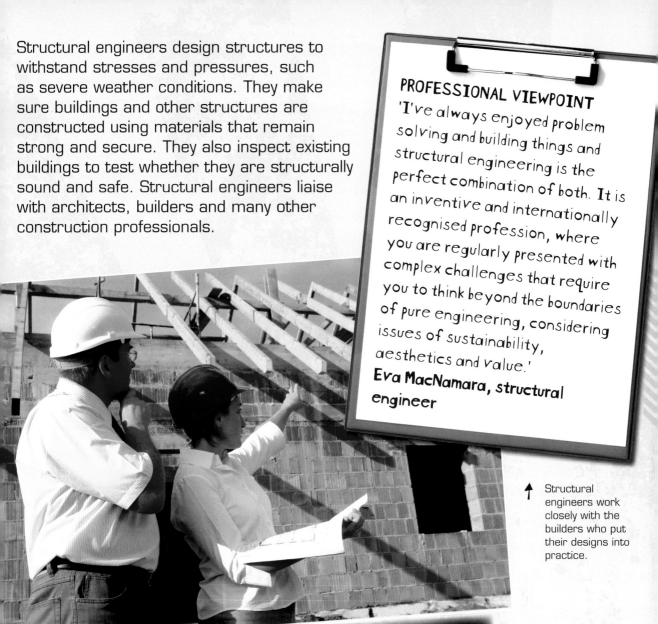

↑ Structural engineers work closely with the builders who put their designs into practice.

# What skills do I need?

You need to be good at maths, physics and IT, and finding solutions to construction problems. You can enter this career at technician level, after studying for a BTEC HNC/HND or an engineering foundation degree, to gain knowledge of construction methods, health and safety, and legal regulations. However, many structural engineers have a degree or Masters (MEng) degree in structural or civil engineering.

# Clinical engineer

Anyone who has ever visited a doctor's surgery, hospital or clinic has probably benefited from the work of clinical engineers. They develop and maintain the technology used to diagnose, help and treat patients, from thermometers and crutches to heart pacemakers.

## PROFESSIONAL VIEWPOINT

'We make sure the right technology is in place, sometimes loaning it out from our library. We train staff, service and mend a huge range of devices, and help develop practical equipment for people with disabilities. We service the medical equipment at a lot of GP practices, and support wheelchair services.'

**Shona Michael, clinical engineer**

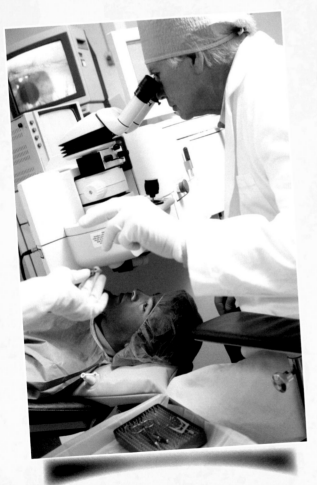

↑ Laser surgery has become commonplace – partly because of the work of clinical engineers in developing laser technology.

## Different types of clinical engineer

Some clinical engineers design and test devices that help disabled people, including walking aids, wheelchairs, hearing aids and speech synthesisers. Others develop artificial hip joints, heart valves and synthetic tissues from new materials. Some clinical engineers design new medical technologies, ranging from laser equipment or optical instruments for keyhole surgery, to new methods of monitoring patients. Clinical engineers collaborate with many other professionals such as doctors, surgeons and material scientists, as well as the patients themselves.

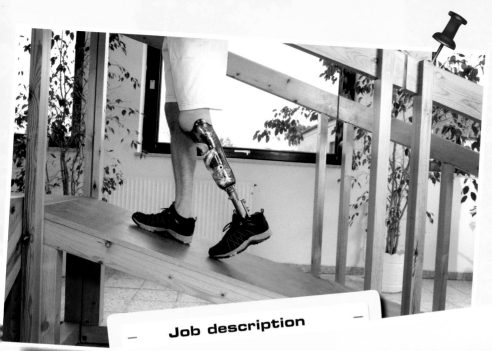

Clinical engineers design the shapes and specifications of artificial limbs to give amputees greater mobility.

## Job description

## Clinical engineers:

- design and test equipment and artificial body parts
- research, develop and use new materials to make artificial body parts
- design equipment that allows doctors to try new medical techniques
- service and repair equipment and make sure it is in the right location when needed
- work closely with other medical professionals, technical staff and patients on a wide range of healthcare technologies.

# What skills do I need?

You need excellent technical knowledge, a keen interest in solving clinical problems and an inventive mind. Most clinical engineers have a degree in a subject such as electrical, electronic or mechanical engineering, or healthcare science. They then train as a clinical scientist, and gain clinical experience in the National Health Service.

# Pattern cutter

If you are interested in fashion, you might like to use your D&T skills to become a pattern cutter. These people create patterns from illustrations created by a fashion designer. The patterns can then be made into samples to see how the final clothes will look.

## Job description

### Pattern cutters:

- refer to a library of patterns to find one that they can adapt into a style
- work closely with fashion designers, interpreting their drawings of clothing designs
- shape, pin and fit pieces of fabric over dummies, and then cut out a pattern based on those pieces
- use a computer to make pattern pieces and templates on fabric, to minimise waste during cutting
- work with machinists to make samples.

← A pattern cutter pins and drapes fabric pieces on a dummy.

## Different types of pattern cutter

Some pattern cutters create pieces that are draped (laid) over a dummy to give an impression of what the garment will look like. Other pattern cutters use computer-generated models to get a sense of how the patterns will look. They may adapt existing patterns of similar garments or design their own. Some pattern cutters are graders. They make scaled-up and scaled-down versions of the patterns to produce the same garment in different sizes.

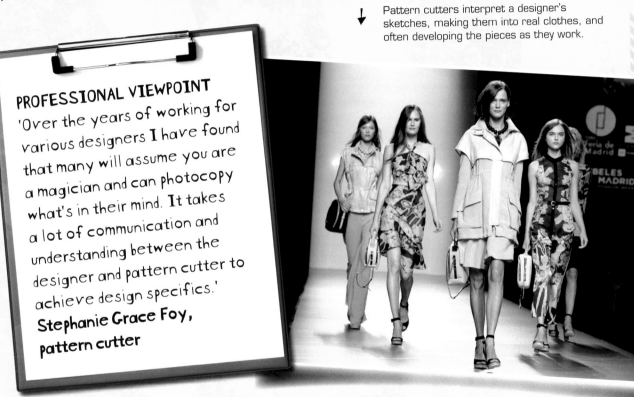

↓ Pattern cutters interpret a designer's sketches, making them into real clothes, and often developing the pieces as they work.

**PROFESSIONAL VIEWPOINT**
'Over the years of working for various designers I have found that many will assume you are a magician and can photocopy what's in their mind. It takes a lot of communication and understanding between the designer and pattern cutter to achieve design specifics.'
**Stephanie Grace Foy, pattern cutter**

# What skills do I need?

Pattern cutters need to be able to work quickly and accurately and have good maths skills for taking measurements and making calculations. They also require sewing, drawing and CAD skills. Many pattern cutters gain their skills by doing a Certificate or Diploma in Fashion and Textiles (Pattern Cutting) or a higher-level course, such as a foundation degree, BTEC HND or a degree in clothing technology and production.

# Machine printer

If you have an eye for design and colour and would like a hands-on, practical job, becoming a machine printer could be for you. Machine printers (sometimes called print minders) set up, operate, maintain and load materials into printing presses.

Printing presses are complicated machines that need to be set up and maintained properly to ensure excellent print results.

## – Job description –

### Machine printers:
- match ink colours to design specification and restock ink levels in machines
- feed the print materials into the presses
- perform colour and quality checks throughout the print run
- identify problems and fix faults
- clean the ink off the presses and printing plates after a print run has finished
- carry out basic machine maintenance.

↑ Machine printers check proofs or sample prints to see if the colour reproduction is accurate.

## Different types of machine printer

Machine printers often specialise in particular printing techniques. Some use flexographic printing to print onto flexible items like shopping bags and food packaging. Others use screen printing (or stencilling) to print designs onto T-shirts, posters or display signs. Lithographic printers often work in teams to operate the massive machines that print newspapers, magazines, leaflets and books in large quantities. Some machine printers use inkjet and laser printing methods.

## What skills do I need?

Most print companies look for a good standard of general education, such as GCSE grades in English, maths, science subjects and IT. Some people become apprentices to printers and also take college printing courses like City & Guilds in Printing and Graphic Communications. Useful skills include practical mechanical abilities and good colour vision.

# Glossary

**architecture**  art and practice of designing buildings, city layouts and other human habitats

**CAD**  computer-assisted design; software used to create technical designs allowing easy modification

**CAM**  computer-aided manufacturing; use of computer software to operate machines that make objects

**computer modelling**  using computer software to make a model of a design, system or plan in order to visualise and test it

**dementia**  loss of mental abilities (such as memory and communication), usually caused by brain disease

**design brief**  document specifying what a design needs to achieve, what materials it will be made from, and how and when it will be completed

**design constraint**  limitation that affects what a design can achieve; for example, a car engine needs to fit into a particular space

**dummy**  model or manikin used to design and construct clothing

**formwork**  temporary or permanent mould used to contain poured concrete

**hazard**  something that could cause harm, such as damaged electrical wires or uneven steps

**high voltage**  powerful electrical force that can make electricity travel over long distances or operate large machines; high voltages can cause especially dangerous electric shocks

**hygiene**  cleanliness and other practices that preserve health, such as washing hands to get rid of bacteria

**keyhole surgery**  operations using special imaging and surgical tools introduced through very small incisions

**pacemaker**  electrical device used to create a steady heartbeat in people with heart problems

**portfolio**  collection of a designer's creative work, demonstrating their abilities

**prototype**  full-scale working model of a design, used to test its capabilities

**properties of materials**  qualities of substances, such as their strength, flexibility, heat-resistance, etc.

**quality controller**  person who maintains quality or standards of production by testing samples and machinery

**recyclability**  suitability of something to be reused as a whole or in part, rather than becoming waste (for example, steel, plastic, glass and tyres in a car can be recycled)

**soldering**  using spots of hot, melted metal mixtures to join metal parts together

**sustainability**  minimising the environmental impact of a product or system during manufacture, use, and after use

**textile**  fabric made from fibres which are generally woven, knitted or bonded together into layers

**wind farm**  group of wind turbines used to generate electricity from the energy in wind

# Further information

There are many specific courses, apprenticeships and jobs using D&T skills, so where do you go to find out more? It is really useful to meet up with careers advisers at school or college and to attend careers fairs to see the range of opportunities. Remember that public libraries and newspapers are other important sources of information. The earlier you check out your options, the better prepared you will be to put your design and technology skills to good use as you earn a living in future.

## Books

*All-New Woodworking for Kids*, Kevin McGuire, Lark, 2008

*Art and Design Activebook: Building the Best Portfolio*, John Davies and Maggie Edwards, Edexcel, 2007

*Building Green Spaces* (Green Collar Careers), Ruth Owen, Crabtree, 2009

*Exploring Package Design* (Design Exploration), Chuck Groth, Delmar Cengage, 2005

*The Teen Vogue Handbook: An Insider's Guide to Careers in Fashion*, Puffin, 2010

*Towering Giants and Other Tall Megastructures*, Ian Graham, QED, 2012

## Websites

**www.bconstructive.co.uk**
This website is worth checking out if you are considering a career in construction, whether it is carpentry, structural engineering or bricklaying.

**www.creative-choices.co.uk/industry-insight**
Read interviews with a range of people in creative careers, many using D&T skills.

**www.designcouncil.org.uk/about-design/How-designers-work/Design-methods**
How do designers come up with ideas and work out if they are any good? You can learn all about prototypes and brainstorming on this website.

**www.designcouncil.org.uk/Case-studies**
The Design Council website includes many fascinating case studies.

**www.greatachievements.org/?id=3824**
Look at the timeline on this website to learn about the history of several health technologies that have significantly improved people's lives.

**www.baddesigns.com/examples.html**
What is bad design? See some examples and suggested solutions here!

# Index

# I'M GOOD AT...

## Contents of all the titles in the series: